Frederick and His Amazing Headphones

Robyn **Heidelberg**
Illustrated by **Gayle Cobb**

Copyright © 2023 by Robyn Heidelberg. All rights reserved.

This book or any portion thereof may not be reproduced or used in any manner whatsoever without the express written permission of the publisher except for the use of brief quotations in a scholarly work or book review. For permissions or further information contact Braughler Books LLC at info@braughlerbooks.com.

Illustrated by Gayle Cobb

Printed in the United States of America

First Printing, 2023

ISBN 978-1-955791-82-3

Library of Congress Control Number: 2023919931

Ordering Information: Special discounts are available on quantity purchases by bookstores, corporations, associations, and others. For details, contact the publisher at sales@braughlerbooks.com or at 937-58-BOOKS.

For questions or comments about this book, please write to info@braughlerbooks.com.

To my sweet Camden, Emma, my mom, my husband, and my teaching team known as the Dino-Mite Teachers.

Camden, my superhero, and son, you are the inspiration for this book especially for all you have gone through. Love you to the moon and back!

Emma, my daughter, my book loving girl, I hope you love reading this book!

My mom, Karen, and my husband, Joe, who always told me to follow my dream! Thanks for supporting me.

Dino-Mite Teachers Team, you are a dino-mite team! The page numbers on every single page are for you!

One warm and sunny day in the Florida Keys, Frederick, his mom, and his dad were off to a restaurant called the Poppin' Pineapple.

"Welcome to the Poppin' Pineapple!" said Hank the host.

"Oh, wait! Hey Frederick! Is it Friday already? I will take you to your usual seat with your mom and dad!"

"Hi Hank! Yes, it is Friday! Our day to come eat," Frederick excitedly exclaimed!

"Here is your seat! Enjoy your Friday dinner!" Hank said.

"Mmmmm, maybe I will try something different. They are known for their Pineapple Pasta which I hear is tasty!" Dad said.

"Frederick, why don't you try the Pineapple Pasta this time?" Mom said very lovingly.

"No, mom. I want what I always get. The kids cheese pizza is the best. It is what I eat here!" Frederick replied.

They ordered their food and of course Frederick ordered his typical cheese pizza! Dad ordered Pineapple Pasta with a side salad and Mom ordered some Poppin' chicken poppers on a salad!

Just as they were about to eat their dinner, a gaggle of geese walked in and sat down at a table across the way from Frederick. They were squawking and honking like crazy because they just won a soccer game!

Suddenly… Frederick throws his wings on his ears and starts freaking out!

"MOM!!!!! It is too LOUD in here!!!" he yells.

While Frederick is yelling, the gaggle of geese start to stare at Frederick.

Frederick's mom quickly grabs his headphones out of her purse and puts them on Frederick.

"You good now?" his mom asks.

"Yes, thanks mom," Frederick says as he gives a thumbs up with a sigh of relief.

One of the geese comes over to Frederick and his family. He asks, "Why does he wear headphones?"

Frederick still has his headphones on and says, "HUH? WHAT?"

"Frederick, lift your headphones up to hear for a minute. It is a little quieter now." Dad says with a chuckle.

"Frederick has a super sensitivity to loud noises. The headphones calm him down and allow him to be able to eat dinner through the noise. He has sensory difficulties or what is called Sensory Processing Disorder," says Frederick's mom.

One of the geese responds with, "That is so interesting! It makes total sense of why you would need the headphones since we were loud when we came in. I am sorry we bothered your dinner. You have some cool headphones!"

"Thanks for asking about my headphones! What is your name?" Frederick asked the goose.

"My name is Gerard! Would you like to be friends? Maybe we can hang out some time together?" Gerard asks.

"S-s-s-s-sure." Frederick says shyly while looking down.

Gerard and Frederick exchange phone numbers.

Frederick's family pays for their meal and walks out of the Poppin' Pineapple. They decide they should end the night with a tasty treat!

Frederick and his family arrive at the Icy Igloo to get some yummy ice cream. Frederick is so excited he quickly gets out of the car and races to the line for ice cream to be first in line. He always wants to be first but is super sad to see he is not first in line. Frederick sees the long line and joins in with his mom and dad.

Frederick starts wiggling and dancing. Then he gets into a craze of spinning! He is spinning and spinning and spinning until…..

PLOP!

"Frederick, are you okay, buddy? I know you love to spin, but you do have trouble knowing when to stop." Dad expresses.

Frederick jumps right up and says, "I am okay!" with a big smile on his face!

After what feels like a lifetime, Frederick has his chocolate milkshake in hand! Frederick and his family jump in the car with ice cream in hand!

"Mom, I am feeling a little bit yellow. I need some help getting back to green." Frederick says.

"Thanks for using your color chart to help us know where you are at when it comes to your needs. Sweetie, was the loudness of the geese and the excitement of ice cream plus meeting a new friend just too much for you?" asks Mom.

"Yes, do you think I could swing in my room to help calm me down?" Frederick asks.

"Sure! You definitely had sensory overload today. Swinging is one way to help get you back to our Frederick who feels green on his chart," says Mom.

Frederick hops on his swing in his bedroom and starts counting his swings, "1…2…3…4…5…"

Frederick is calming down and definitely feeling more ready for bedtime, so he continues to count, "6…7…8…9…"

Then the phone rings!

Sensory Processing Disorder/Sensory Processing Difficulties

Sensory processing difficulties is when one of the areas of our senses causes difficulty to function in everyday life. People with sensory processing difficulties can be over-responsive and under-responsive to a specific sense. Sensory processing is when you have trouble processing an area of one of our senses and it causes a certain behavior. For example, loud music in a movie theater may cause a child to cover their ears and scream. It can also cause the child not to be able to focus. The way the child may need to get through loud noises is using noise canceling headphones or using headphones that play relaxing music.

The five senses that everyone knows easily are touch, smell, taste, sight, and hearing. In all reality, there are 8 types of senses. They include auditory (sound), visual (sight), Olfactory (smell), Gustatory (taste), Tactile (touch), Vestibular (balance), Proprioceptive (movement), and Interoceptive (feeling).

- **Difficulties with Auditory (Sound):** Children with auditory difficulties may be startled by unexpected or loud sounds, ears can be super sensitive to sounds, trouble focusing in loud or noisy environments, easily distracted, misunderstanding jokes or sarcasm, and anxiety in noisy situations, sounds may cause meltdowns, can hear noises that most people don't hear, and it can cause them not to focus or fixate on it such as a refrigerator humming

- **Difficulties with Visual (sight):** difficulty keeping eye contact, sensitivity to light especially bright lights, can lose place when reading, can be overwhelmed with word searches or puzzles, can have trouble finding something in a room or a place
- **Difficulties with Olfactory (smell):** this one can go one of two ways- under-responsive which is where the child smells everything including nonfood items, over-responsive where the child is overwhelmed by smells which can cause a meltdown
- **Difficulties with Gustatory (taste):** avoids foods with specific taste or texture, sometimes they only focus on a specific texture they like such as crunchy foods or mushy foods and can avoid the undesired textures, anxiety can happen when having to try new foods, they can crave a specific strong flavor or temperature of food; can also be sensitive and think food is hot when it seems cool to others, licking or chewing inedible food
- **Difficulties with Tactile (touch):** children can avoid the following: brushing teeth, taking baths, certain textures of clothing can cause anxiety, haircuts, clipping nails, hugging or touch by someone else
- **Difficulties with Vestibular (balance):** clumsiness, rocking back and forth, frequent motion sickness, pacing, head banging, resistance to move, unaware of physical danger in certain situations such as climbing everything or jumping off things, etc.

- **Difficulties with Proprioceptive (movement):** difficulty isolating body movements, misjudge amount of force needed to lift objects (may break things unintentionally), frequent kicking when sitting, frequent stomping when walking, playing too rough with others, not knowing when they are dizzy when spinning
- **Difficulties with Interoceptive (feeling):** poor understanding of when to eat or drink, struggling to feel pain or temperature, not knowing when to use the restroom (can be harder to potty train), does not understand basic feelings of others or personally

Sensory Processing Disorder or Difficulties is not an official medical disorder on the DSM-5. Most medical professionals diagnose it with something else and diagnose it as difficulties.

For more information you may visit the Star Institute: https://sensoryhealth.org/

Citations:

Covey (n.d.). *Sensory Processing Disorder: How the 8 Senses Affect Behavior*. Retrieved January 15, 2023, from https://covey.org/sensory-processing-disorder/?utm_source=google&utm_medium=cpc&utm_campaign=030422_GoogleGrant_SensoryProcessingDisorder&gclid=CjwKCAiA5Y6eBhAbEiwA_2ZWIeGcZuiXwMXJjV4fpZkLuAQrNJT0RHPJcQ1n7ff8tyH5zyOzRhKmChoCIfYQAvD_BwE

About the Author

Robyn Heidelberg is a first-grade teacher and mother of a child with Sensory Processing Disorder (SPD). She has been teaching for 14 years as a classroom teacher of elementary students which have consisted of first or third graders over the years. She has a bachelor's degree in early childhood education and a master's degree in literacy and second language. She has experience of working with students who have sensory difficulties in the classroom and at home in her personal life. Robyn lives with her husband, son, and daughter.

Frederick and His Amazing Headphones is in honor of her son and just a small part of what her son, Camden, has gone through with sensory processing. Camden has experienced the difficulty of loud noises out in public and having to wear headphones. Many people wonder or are curious why his headphones are used. Camden's headphones can keep him calm in many situations! Robyn wrote this book in hopes to help spread awareness on SPD, so children and their families don't feel alone. She wanted children to have a book character to be able to connect with. Robyn wants this to be read in classrooms as well to help explain why a student may wear headphones.

www.ingramcontent.com/pod-product-compliance
Lightning Source LLC
Chambersburg PA
CBHW061418090426
42743CB00022B/3484